Dzogchen
Elements of Daily Ritual Practice

Keith Dowman

Dzogchen Now! Books
2020

Dzogchen Now! Books

www.keith.dowman.net

ISBN: 9798689195858

Printed in Goudy Old Style 12pt

Contents

I

Introduction

To some it may seem strange to see a radical Dzogchen text entitled Daily Ritual Practice. The first principle of radical Dzogchen is the assumption of the perfection of the here and now wherever we are and in whatever condition we find ourselves. That understanding was indelibly set in our being and in our minds upon the initial realization of the *nature* of mind, and it gave an extraordinary breadth and depth to life.

Many of us, however, find ourselves in the habit of sitting at a fixed place and for a fixed time once or twice every day to perform the ritual of *trekcho* or *togal*. Others are inclined to sit but have not found a satisfactory routine. For all these Dzogchen so-called practitioners it is imperative to have sloughed off the impulse to improve or enlighten themselves. We cannot enter the immediate path of Dzogchen until we have intuited the complete futility in the striving on a graduated path. Only then can the graduated path be integrated into the immediate path so that the immediate path can be realized. That is another way of saying that the unitary pathless path is achieved by initiatory experience into the nature of mind.

When formal sitting-meditation free of directed motivation is performed with as little concern as taking a shower after getting out of bed in the morning we are experiencing that most anticipated Dzogchen mindset, careless and free. In order to be effectual the simply sitting Dzogchen mode should have no greater importance or value than any other activity of the daily round, which is to not to debase Dzogchen but rather to realize the crucial, vital, status of every moment of the day and to have imbued every instant of the complete 24-hours with the Dzogchen ethos. By all means include a ritual sitting practice, but Dzogchen initiatory experience has taught us the lesson that the nature of mind and enlightened attitude are inherent in all physical, energetic and mental activity. Evidence of realization is the experience of every moment of the 24-hours as of equal worth. That experience provides the rationale for calling radical Dzogchen meditation 'nonmeditation'.

It is only with the understanding that simply sitting is nonmeditation that we can properly engage in formal meditation. Once we have that understanding, free of any impulse towards enlightenment or at least disabused of the folly that we can actually prepare the ground for buddha, only then can we simply sit. It should be stressed now that these remarks are only valid in the Dzogchen context – other traditions have a less lofty view and more pedestrian aims, goals that can be attained by the causal meditation that can surely improve the relative state of being.

The essence of the daily ritual practice of non-meditation is simply sitting. The practice of simply sitting is called a 'ritual', but that should be understood in the context of the Dzogchen view in which the entire 24-hours of the day is known as ritual. This insight arises out of the initiatory experience of mind's nature. When we identify either existentially or conceptually with the nature of mind, whatever occurs, physically, energetically or mentally, in body speech or mind, is a ritual symbolizing mind's nature. Of course, whatever we do has conventional meaning and purpose; it has karmic volition, a cause and an effect; but putting that aside whatever we do is a ritual manifestation at once embodying and pointing at the nature of mind. Such a ritual consumes everyone who has had full experience of mind's nature and whose only purpose in life is to retain identity with the essence of being. That implies enjoyment of the ritual of embodiment. To put it another way, we are identified with nondual awareness to enjoy the illusory duality of karmic propensity.

The ritual of life is well expressed in the buddhist tantric epigram: 'sitting, eating, walking, shitting', and the grossness emphasizes one of the didactic themes of the epigram. We are conditioned to believe that the subtle is in some way superior to the gross; we have the 'intellectuals' and the 'aesthetes' and the 'mystics' based in the folly of refinement when the awareness that is the ultimate cultural refinement is also found – and equally – in the football crowd, in sexual debauch, in the army barracks or indeed in battle itself. There are no degrees or levels of karmic purity: 'karma' is karma of the human soul, every manifestation of human life uniformly rooted in the nature of mind. The wheel of life constantly spins, taking us through both upper and lower realms, and all states of mind, surely, are equally illusory and equally sticky.

An intuitive grasp of life as ritual integrates daily practice into everyday life: simply sitting practice is not distinct from the vicissitudes arising in the gaps between simply sitting periods. Freed from the need to produce any result from meditation, the elements of practice become a source and expression of pleasure. The buddhas, wrathful or peaceful, are always inherent in the unitary here and now, never to be confronted in a 'me'-and-'it' dualization. The wrathful deities in the mandala are integrated as compassionate clowns with terrific faces and costumes. The yab-yum pairs are locked into a basic understanding of mutual awareness. The imps and goblins at the mandala's periphery are sympathetic figures of fun. We play life as a dance of either peace or war, tragedy or comedy, sexual harmony or belligerent conflict, but always as illusionary show intrinsic within the complete and perfect unitary Dzogchen moment.

Thus simply sitting is a product of initiatory experience, rather than a cause of it. To simply sit with the express purpose of relieving the pain of existence is counter-productive – there are other better ways of reducing anxiety. Simply sitting is performed without any purpose at all. Initiatory experience has convinced us that the nature of mind is perfect as it stands and that whatever arises out of it , likewise, is as perfect as can be, and that nothing whatsoever can be done to improve it. Meditation guilds the lily; nonmeditation appreciates the natural flower.

If simply sitting has not been drained of every trace of ambition or aspiration we are back to the causal vehicles (Hinayana or Mahayana), or perhaps to the Vajrayana where the pretense of initiatory experience or the mere form of ritual initiation leaves the aspirant hanging in a purgatory of unfulfilled expectation. So long as there is a suggestion – even a hint – of anticipation or hope, a prospect of improvement, 'a better rebirth', 'enlightenment' in the future, daily practice and simply sitting are undercut and may prove counterproductive. We are looking at the total disillusionment – demonstrated in European Existentialism – infused by the nature of mind and then realized in psychedelic experience, Tibetan or chemical. It is with this background, in this context, that the elements of Daily Ritual Practice can be most profitably assimilated.

I Elements of Practice

Primary Elements

Simply sitting

Simply sitting is shorthand for what we call nonmeditation in radical Dzogchen. It is identical to the practice of *trekcho*, which is a technical name for the approach to simply sitting. Simply sitting is the essential practice as it entertains no directed activity whatsoever and is therefore a blueprint for the 24-hour-a-day exercise and clarification of nonmeditation.

Refuge and Celebration

The daily Dzogchen ritual is essentially simply sitting. However, as in all ritual processes, it has a beginning middle and end. The beginning consists of the Nine Breaths, the Refuge and Celebration (of the Bodhisattva Vow). The rituals of Refuge and Bodhisattva Vow appear at the commencement of all Mahayoga and Anuyoga practices, and are of no less importance in Dzogchen Atiyoga. Insofar as they appear at the start of the ritual they are of primary importance and should not be overlooked as vocal impediments. The Refuge is a reminder of initiatory experience, the refuge in which we are naturally and inescapably embedded. We were part of it before birth and we are a part of it after death and, in this life, we are rooted in it. We have never left it and the Refuge is a ritual recognition of that fact.

In radical Dzogchen Refuge is expressed not in discursive vocal form but in the symbolic sound HŪNG. HŪNG is the seed-syllable of the heart-center. When we require further confirmation that our refuge is indeed present as the here and now, we can add *sotto voce* the discursive formula, 'We abide in the nature of mind that is our refuge.' We use the first-person-plural to include all sentient beings because whether we recognize it or not everyone is identified with the nature of mind and cannot leave it, and it is useful to recall that often. The word 'refuge' was a term coined in the Hinayana and used in the Mahayana where going for refuge in Buddha, Dharma and Sangha is seen as an escape from the perils of samsara into nirvana, and in the Vajrayana refuge is found in the guru-lama. Radical Dzogchen leaves this provisional terminology behind after recognition of mind's nature. Now, we take refuge in the nature of mind where buddha is clear light, dharma is the spectrum of color, and sangha sensory experience.

Following the Refuge, Celebration of the Bodhisattva Vow is expressed as the syllable **HO**! Consciousness of the celebratory aspect of being accompanies the Refuge and suffuses the entire ritual procedure. Implicit in the elation and felicity of recognition of the nature of mind is the open-heartedness that includes all sentient beings, and thus expresses existentially the bodhisattva vow that is expressed as 'We recognize the spontaneous expression of mind's nature as fulfilment of the bodhisattva vow.' In this way we celebrate the enlightened mind and its implicit intent to do whatsoever is necessary for the sake of all sentient beings. Thereby we express discursively the universal presence of *bodhichitta*, enlightened mind, and our understanding that it is implicit in whatever we do.

Supportive Elements

The Dzogchen *ngondro* practices are best conceived as a lubricant that allows the smooth and automatic functioning of spontaneous nondual perception. It is like playing musical scales before the concert; like a kick-about warm-up before the ball game; like foreplay before sex. If we are totally in sync with the action then we don't need foreplay, but we can nevertheless indulge in it as ritual pleasure of a different kind.

There is a danger of treating the elements of the *ngondro* as stepping stones necessary to get to the place where we can actualize the nature of mind. It is counter-productive to the Dzogchen project to see the *ngondro* as preliminary to an understanding of the nature of mind. The concept of *ngondro* as a first stage practice and then application of effort over a tenderfoot period of practice is to sink onto a mire of quicksand and lose altogether the essential Dzogchen initiatory ethos of 'perfect in the here and now'. *Ngondro* is indeed an expression of the nature of mind; the danger counteracted here is of conceiving it as a preliminary practice and becoming attached to it on a gradual path.

Dzogchen abandons the idea of *ngondro* as preliminary grounding. It lets go of the *ngondro* as an exercise in removing gross obstacles from the path, lets go the idea of the path as a linear progression from start to finish, from samsara to nirvana, darkness into light. Right from the beginning we let go of the idea of Dzogchen as a graduated path. Then we can include it as a prelude even more engaging than the symphony itself.

The supportive *ngondro* elements can be usefully called *clarification practices.*

Clarification of Body: Vajra Standing Posture

The vajra-standing-posture is a salutary reminder to the Dzogchen yogi that the physical body is the vessel and the home of the more subtle energetic and mental dimensions and if only for that reason it should be practiced assiduously. The body is the ground and as such can be included totally in the spaciousness of mind. That is an intelligent approach for the yogin who spends his life in the unitary space of the nondual mind. The posture itself is physically difficult, energetically taxing and mentally demanding for anyone who is not in the peak of health, but it should be practiced by all. After rigorous practice that has made it second nature it can be included in the daily ritual.

The vajra is the tantric vehicle to buddha – the Vajrayana. In poor translation it is 'indestructible' or 'adamantine', but it is the one adjective that adequately describes the nature of mind, which, of course, has no substance or attribute.

Clarification of Speech: HŪNG *Breathing*

The HŪNG breathing should be considered simply as 'conscious breathing', 'breathing with full awareness'. Conscious breathing is done with marginally longer inbreath and outbreath but otherwise the breathing process is normal. What distinguishes Dzogchen breathing is the potentiation of the awareness inherent in ordinary breathing and the psychological shift that occurs from mental thought-preoccupation to heightened perceptual and energetic cognition. To go straight to the optimal result of the exercise: the visual field becomes a mandala of heightened perception of illusory rainbow-colored phenomena, and insofar as that mandala is free of mentally-projected definition in name and form, it is a very happy picture.

A detailed description of the visualization is provided in the extended summation below, but the essence — or magic — of the exercise lies in the symbolic value of the HŪNGs. The syllable HŪNG is 'charged' in the Vajrayana practice of mantra recitation and as a potent seed-syllable in Mahayana visualization, but in Dzogchen realization it is identified with the nature of mind. Thus, when we visualize a cloud of HŪNGs carried on the breath, we are investing the energetic phenomena of the breath with mind's nature and in the process liberating the senses from karmic corruption or interference. The color here is of crucial importance: sky blue evokes the spaciousness that dissolves boundaries while red inspires the heat and flames of demolition that destroy all sense of the material and substantial. Dissolution of the sense of both macro and micro, external and internal substantiality are required before the unitary field of illusory phenomena arises.

Stick Climbing HŪNGs

Visualizing the train of blue-black stick-climbing HŪNGs emanating from the heart-center to spiral up and down a stick standing in front is an element of the *ngondro* taken from Yogi Chen, a disciple of Dudjom Rinpoche. It constitutes a pig in a poke in *ngondro* practices. In order to sustain the dynamic visualization, we need to be truly identified with the nature of mind. If the rational mind is still in gear, then we will focus on a single aspect of the exercise – a single HŪNG, the stick, or the train of HŪNGs spiraling either up or down, or upon any single element of the visualization – rather than the totality of dynamic elements moving within a static frame. The visualization is akin to a consciously-imagined daydream, or to watching a movie playing in your head. In this way it is a litmus test of our capacity to identify with the ground of awareness.

Further, if we consider the elements of the visualization in relation to the heart-center (*chakra*) and the central channel (*avadhuti*) we see a model of the process of manifestation out of the nondual core into the creative and destructive aspects of being. The blue-black color indicates a wholly dynamic picture reminiscent of the protecting-deity Mahankal (Mahakala).

Clarification of Mind

In this present Dzogchen context 'mind' is to be defined as consciousness of the processes of thought and emotion (leaving out its various super-psychological functions). The clarification of mind is then to be achieved by looking for the mind, at the mind and into the mind. First, define the mind as thought and emotion and attempt to pin it down. In the second stage, by identifying specific thoughts and feelings we are in the process of identifying with them even as we gain cognizance of them. Finally, we look into the nature of the thought and/or emotion, or to put it another way, we look at the nature of mind.

Trying to pin down, objectively, the constituents of a constant process of change, whether that is thought or emotion, is an exercise in futility. But in that process the thinker is notionally detached from the thought, and the-one-who-feels is detached from the emotion, and in the lessening of attachment our neuroses dissolve and the sky begins to clear.

Gazing at the nature of mind leaves us at the very place we need to fully engage in the simply sitting. Or perhaps we are utilizing the clarification of mind, *ngondro,* to regain the mindset we need to continue with the twenty-four hour a day nonmeditation.

Guru and Preceptor

In Dzogchen the Guru is the nature of mind and the preceptor is the teacher who points out the nature of mind. In the Vajrayana tradition the Guru is incarnate as the lama-teacher, and insofar as the Tibetan teacher of Dzogchen is the Vajrayana lama who provides the Dzogchen ritual initiation *(rigpaitsel-wong)*, in practice the Tibetan preceptor is the Vajrayana Guru. In distinction from common Indian usage where the guru is every kind of teacher, let's keep the term Guru for the mystical initiator into the tantric tradition – the one Guru is Guru Rinpoche who appears in various and multifarious forms.

Thus, my Guru is Guru Rinpoche, the nature of mind manifest as my preceptors Dudjom Rinpoche and Kanjur Rinpoche, who were both 'white-shawled' students of Trinle Jampa Jungne, a Khampa Lama born in the mid-19th century. They both represent the long temporal lineage, stretching out of the mists of time from the root-guru Garab Dorje down to the Khampa representatives in the refugee exodus from Tibet in the 1960s. This long lineage extending over some fifteen hundred years is composed of individuals who realized the nature of mind through initiatory experience, either immediate or graduated. With experience of the nature of mind in common, each comprised a link in a temporal lineage confirming the experience of his/her preceptor.

The short lineage is the nontemporal lineage stemming from Samantabhadra (Kuntuzangpo) in the unitary *dharmakaya*, through Vajrasattva (Dorjesempa) in the *sambhogakaya*, into our *nirmanakaya* represented as Guru Rinpoche. In the short lineage the nature of mind is defined as our three existential aspects, the *trikaya*.

We belong to both these lineages, the long and short. The short provides the crucial existential identity with mind's nature and is proven in the initiatory experience that provides intuition of complete identity. The long lineage, an Atiyoga linage, ties us to a tradition of temporal incarnation-in-the-world that in its very personality-diversity emphasizes the formlessness – the utter non-existence – of the nature of mind that links us. If we arrived at Dzogchen through Vajrayana then our Dzogchen preceptor will probably be our Vajrayana

Guru. In that case be sure that the graduated path has been imbued with immediate path ethos!

An automatic connection with the short linage is made through initiatory experience. Connection with the long lineage is also made thereby, verbal exhortation providing names and forms. The short lineage reality is confirmed by long lineage personality. Internally we may be existentially certain of the absolute nondual nature of being, but socially, in relation to others, we cannot confirm our own understanding without affirming a 'self' or an 'ego' that makes that confirmation and for that reason long-lineage endorsement is vital.

II Dzogchen Meditation Sessions

The Short Essential Session

Homage to Samantabhadra!

Nine Breaths

Nine deep breaths, emptying the lungs, fully filling the lungs, three exhalations from the left nostril, three from the right nostril, three from both nostrils. And rest easy.

Refuge

HŪNG ! (thrice)

Optional: **We abide in the nature of mind that is our refuge.** And rest easy.

Celebration: Bodhisattva Vow

HO! (thrice)

Optional: **We recognize the spontaneous expression of mind's nature as fulfilment of the bodhisattva vow.** And rest easy.

Simply Sitting

Trekcho nonmeditation: the following indications are not necessarily progressive in development and all are essentially synonymous:

Watching the nature of mind
relaxing into the natural state of being
bringing the mind back home
resting in the nature of mind
resting, relaxing, doing nothing
sustaining the 360-degree perspective

abiding in the nature of mind
being the awareness – ('I am the awareness')
being without fabrication of 'body', 'speech' or 'mind'
without accepting or rejecting,
without cultivating or demolishing
without approval or denial
being in non-discrimination
without intention and without goal
letting it be, just as it is
hanging loosely
in nonaction,
doing nothing.

The syllable PHAT!
Loudly voice the syllable PHAT to evoke the nature of mind whenever appropriate.

Dedication
We dedicate the virtue of this practice to the realization of the great perfection in all sentient beings.

The Long Inclusive Session:

Elements of Dzogchen: Ritual Practice of Trekcho

The Nine Breaths
Settle in and sit comfortably.
Take the seven-point stance of Vairochana.
Eye mudra: wide open, gazing straight ahead.
Deep breaths emptying the lungs and then filling and stretching the lungs (vase breathing), three from the left

nostril, three from the right nostril, three from both nostrils. And rest easy.

Refuge

HŪNG ! (thrice)

Optional: **We abide in the nature of mind that is our refuge.** And rest easy.

[Include the Four Immeasurables, sing the refuge song when available]

Celebration: Bodhisattva Vow

HO! (thrice)

Optional: **We recognize the spontaneous expression of mind's nature as fulfilment of the bodhisattva vow.** And rest easy

Guru-yoga

In the sky in front, just above the line of sight, visualize a bubble of light, and sitting in that sphere is Samantabhadra (Kuntuzangpo) the naked, translucent blue, primordial All-Good Buddha. A ray of blue light streams from his heart-center to our own heart center, saturating, clarifying, illuminating, empowering our entire being. Samantabhadra then dissolves into blue light that streams into your heart-center and dissolves into yourself.

Clarification Practices

'Preferably at dawn and dusk, at the time of changing light, perhaps on a prominence in nature, or inside a room before an altar or shrine, take your seat on a cushion, in vajra-posture.'

Clarification of Body

The Three-Pointed Vajra Standing Posture

To mimic the symbolic vajra (*dorje*) stand on your toes with the heals supporting each other, bend the knees to imitate the vajra's lower forks, pull the chin into the neck, and raise the arms above the head with palms together to imitate the vajra's upper forks. Breathe deeply filling the body with energy (*prana*). Visualize the body first as sky-blue in color and then as bright red, haloed in flame. Murmur the syllable HŪNG under the breath.

Clarification of Speech: Purification of Energy and the Energy Field.

The HŪNG breathing takes two forms blue and red:

The Blue HŪNGs

Sitting in vajra-posture, visualize in the torso a large sky-blue HŪNG, and emanating from that HŪNG a cloud of sky-blue HŪNGs of all sizes mixed with the breath and powerfully exhaled in a lengthened outbreath. Of the cloud of HŪNGs, separate HŪNGs vanish into the structures, the bodies, the objects in the immediate visual field, mellowing, gentling, and dissolving their substantiality and perceived form. Eventually we will be looking at a realm of pure color and shape, the visual field suffused with light. In an open field, the blue HŪNGs may enter into both the nano-realm and macro-realm.

Then, on the inbreath mix the breath with the mind and retract the HŪNGs into the large blue HŪNG in the torso. From the HŪNG in the torso a myriad of small s HŪNGs vanish into the internal parts of the body: into the organs – heart, lungs, liver, kidneys, brain and glands and so on – and the vascular and nervous systems. Every cell in the body contains a tiny blue HŪNG, and the HŪNGs populating the body dissolve its substantiality so that each inbreath transforms the body into a body of blue light.

The Red HŪNGs

Then changing the color of the large HŪNG in the torso to bright red, visualize the cloud of HŪNGs emanating from it on the outbreath burning like coals. When projected into the visual field they burn but do not consume the structure, bodies, objects of the macrocosm and microcosm that they enter. Burning away the fabric of existence, they dissolve all materiality, substantiality, leaving only empty, colorful, radiance.

Retracting the red HŪNG s on the inbreath into the source HŪNG in the torso, visualize tiny red HŪNGs dispersed by the source HŪNG entering into the internal constituents of the body and burning but not consuming its organs and subtle physical systems until the entire inner-body is burning, its materiality dissolved.

Continue this HŪNG breathing for some minutes then let the visualization fade away. In an extension of this visualization, project the outbreath beyond your proximate space into the outside environment, into the surrounding dwellings, or into the natural environment. A further extension allows projection of the

HŪNGs beyond the immediate environment into the county.

Flying Vajras: Blue and Red

Visualize a sky-blue colored vajra the size of a thumb-joint standing in the heart-center. Let it move within a spatial extension of the heart-center so that it flies freely around the body passing through every organ and every cell before returning to the heart-center.

Then visualize the blue vajra moving out of the space of the heart-center and out of the body to move around the internal space of the room and the objects and beings within it until it has passed through the entire volume of the room, before returning to the heart-center. Allow it to take whatever course it automatically takes in its passage throughout the room.

Visualizing a flaming bright-red vajra in the heart-center, as before let it explore the body moving throughout its organs and cellular structure, incinerating the substantiality before returning to the heart-center.

Likewise, as before, visualize the bright-red flaming vajra moving from the heart-center to move around the room, passing through every square centimeter, incinerating, desubstantializing, before returning to the heart-center.

Blue-black HŪNGs

Visualize a finger-joint sized blue-black HŪNG in the heart-center and a white stick thirty centimeters (12") long standing in the space in the front at a distance of half a meter (20"). Emanating from the HŪNG in the heart-center visualize an endless train of small blue-black HŪNGs marching to the bottom of the stick and then climbing the stick in a spiral movement to the top and then spiraling down the stick and back to the heart-center, endlessly. Maintain this entire visualization in a single frame without focusing on any part of the train.

Clarification of Mind

1. Cognitively search for the mind: where is it? what is its shape? what is its color? Continue in this search until you come to a definitive pragmatic/experiential (rather than discursive-intellectual) conclusion.

2. Watch your thoughts: what is their source? what is their nature? where do they dissolve?

Watch your emotions: from where do they arise? what are their nature? what is their color? into what do they dissolve?

3. Look into thought as it arises; look at the nature of the thought when it is fully arisen; look at its state of dissolution as it vanishes.

4. Determine existentially what comes first, body, speech or mind. Do external circumstances form a synergy that generates a mental response? Do mental constructs or preconceptions produce an energetic response that generates activity? Is it energetic demand that generates both thought and action? Who is the leader, the physical, energetic, or mental department? Solve this koan and rest in its solution.

Simply Sitting

Trekcho nonmeditation: the following list of instruction may be progressive in development.

Watching the nature of mind
bringing the mind back home
resting in the nature of mind
relaxing in the natural state of being
resting, relaxing, doing nothing
sustaining the 360-degree perspective
abiding in the nature of mind
being the awareness – ('I am the awareness')
being without fabrication of 'body', 'speech' or 'mind'
without accepting or rejecting,
without cultivating or demolishing
without approval or denial
being in non-discrimination
without intention, without goal
letting it be, just as it is
hanging loosely
in nonaction
doing nothing.

In pure presence, in the here and now, do not try to change anything, or to add or subtract anything; but without elaborating or concentrating, just let it be. Neither existence nor nonexistence nor space-time is discoverable. Appearances and emptiness are indistinguishable, so that neither eternity nor the void are anywhere perceptible. In this indefinable space no conceptual view or directed meditation is applicable.

The Four Modes of Freely Resting

Like a mountain and like the ocean, and as appearances and as pure presence (*rigpa*): these are the four modes of freely resting (*chokzhak zhi*) that characterize mind in the natural state of being. To reiterate, 'doing nothing' in *trekcho* nonmeditation may be illustrated by the mountain that is immovable; the ocean that has no center or circumference, peaceful in its depths and alternately smooth and rough on its surface; and as physical, energetic and mental appearance that has no substance and are free of conceptual frame; and as pure presence in which pristine awareness and the forms of appearance are one. (See *Dzogchen Training Series 2: Dzogchen Nonmeditation* pp.16ff)

The syllable PHAT!

Loudly voice the syllable **PHAT** to evoke the nature of mind; to decimate an intractable sensory or mental object; to cut short a thought train; or to dissolve an emotional block.

Dedication

We dedicate the virtue of this practice to the realization of the great perfection.

III Supplementary Ritual

These additional practices are supportive exercises designed as antidotes to obstacles that repeatedly appear and obstinately remain, refusing integration into the view through nonmeditation.

The Semdzin of Emotion

Turning the Five Poisons into the Path

Whatever colors you have in your mind, identify their emotional character and gaze into their empty nature:

Turning the five poisons into the path is a function of primal awareness. The manner of engagement is not to reject desire, anger, sloth, pride, jealousy and so on, but rather to nurture the five poisons as reflexively-released pure presence.

When you recall and relive the harm that an enemy has previously inflicted upon you, such as stealing from you, injuring you or embarrassing and shaming you, hatred rises intensely. As that hatred arises, you look deeply into it to see where – not why but where – it comes from, where it resides (in the upper or lower part of the body, for example), and, finally, where it goes. You look for the color and shape of the hatred, and what that color or shape may be. Failing to find anything substantial you see it, however, as primordially empty, self-less envisionment, and you do not seek to abandon it, because it is mirror-like awareness.

Memory of a former attractive lover may arise: you are drinking liquor and eating meat together, wearing designer fashion and jewelry, recalling riding together, or traveling by car or airplane, and therein remembering the sexual desire. As the desire arises, you are gazing at it nakedly, looking at the place in the body it comes from, where it resides, and, finally, where it goes to. Looking at it, you see its color and shape, but finally, you see it with detachment as primordially empty envisionment, and you do not abandon it because it is discriminating awareness.

You feel sleepy, in decline, in a state of dullness, gloom or depression – in short, the mind is not clear. It is imperceptive and bewildered; it is like a frozen computer. Let the sloth arise! As it arises, you gaze at it carefully: whose sloth is it? where is it coming from? in which part of the body is it to be found? and, finally where is it going to? Does it have color and shape? or any attributes at all? Now, you are looking at it with detachment and it is primordially empty envisionment. Never abandon it – essentially it is awareness of vast spaciousness!

Then thinking of your race, remembering your social status, recalling your bank account and cash-in-hand, musing upon your fine bone structure, the power of your voice, dwelling upon your virtues and positive qualities, pride is arising. In the full flourish of pride gazing at the naked proud one, where does the pride come from? in which part of the body does it exist? and, finally, where does it go to? Does it have color, shape, or any other attribute. You see that ultimately it is primordially empty self-envisionment, and preferring not to abandon it, it becomes awareness of sameness.

Thinking of someone with great wealth, knowledge, fame, privilege, opportunity and so forth, comparing him or her with yourself, jealousy is erupting. Letting it flow, just look at it fixedly: who is the owner of the jealousy? where is it coming from? where does it presently exist in the body? and finally where does it go to? Does it have color, shape or attribute? Seeing that it is primordially empty envisionment, not abandoning it, it is all-accomplishing awareness.

Realizing the nature of any of the emotions, it becomes one of the various modes of awareness. On the flip-side of the errant thoughts that arise with emotion you discover empty awareness – and what a joy that is! If you search for it, however, you cannot find it, and you become pathetically hopeless. You understand primarily that all of the five emotional poisons are baseless and rootless and empty and therefore cannot be pinned. Later, knowing this, when you are engaged on the temporal path, during the gaps between sessions of meditation, whatever thoughts and emotions arise you remain at ease with them, without any need to examine their nature, their origin, their place of abiding, or their place of dissolution. You have no need to examine their shape, color or attribute: the emotion and accompanying thoughts effortlessly disappear by themselves.

In this analysis, both the introduction to the view and the maturation of meditation are complete. For beginners in Dzogchen this sequence of examination, fixation and establishment, and of introduction and maturation, is very effective in dissolving obstacles in simply sitting. Later, automatically, you recognize the nature of whatever emotional poison emerges as it arises and releases simultaneously, repeatedly. Then in your own experience you can clearly see the inexpressible pure presence as the dharmakaya.

Essential Pith Precepts: Semdzins

Before incorporating any of these semdzins into the daily ritual they should have been practiced deeply and extensively. To integrate them into the practice session they should be brought to the point where no discursive, manipulative thought is required for their application. The brief description of the various supportive practices is included here to serve as reminders. (For extensive commentary and explanation see Dzogchen Training Series 2: Dzogchen Semdzins.)

The Semdzin of the Syllable PHAT
When you get tired exclaim the syllable PHAT: sometimes let consciousness run free and then forcefully enunciate the syllable PHAT. A state of thoughtless amazement will arise and until another intractable thought arises the mind is known as pure presence (*rigpa*). Whenever a thought does not automatically dissolve enunciate the syllable PHAT. Experiencing this night and day the meditation of empty luminous mind in its natural condition arises.

The Semdzin of the Heruka's Joyful Laughter

Joyfully laugh the exclamation HA, short and forcefully (start with one and increase to five), and as with the exclamation PHAT the mind is secured and the experience of thoughtfree clarity arises.

The Semdzin of the Long and Short HŪNGs *or the Thought-Pursuing* HŪNGs
Identify long resonant vocalized HŪNGs with the outbreath and when intractable thoughts or thought-trains arise use the short exclamation HŪNG to disperse them. Unmoving from your original condition, clarity of the nature of thought arises.

The Semdzin of the Deity's Body
Visualize oneself as Vajrasattva; visualize Vajrasattva on the tip of the nose, mix him with the outbreath and inbreath; visualize an infinite number of Vajrasattvas in the pores of the skin and the nine bodily orifices emanated on the inbreath and absorbed on the outbreath. With an attentive mind the experience of the consciousness of magnificent pure luminosity arises.

The Semdzin of the Rainbow Body
Visualize a small white 'A' in the heart-center and focus unwaveringly on a net of five-color rainbow light – translucent, clear, insubstantial – emanating from it in all directions, bounded by the sphere in which you sit. You experience the pure clear light.

The Semdzin of Ear Consciousness
Focus attention in the ear and relax. Thereby you will experience the samadhi of sound.

The Semdzin of Kuntuzangpo in the Heart-Center
Focus on the tiny form of Kuntuzangpo (Samantabhadra) in a globe of blue light in the heart-center.

Thereby you will experience pure clear light, and you will cultivate the clear light of the bardo, and at death there is buddha deity, relics (*ringsel*) and rainbow light.

The Semdzin of Union
At the arising of dualistic appearances (subject/object, inside/outside) gaze intently at the crux (totality) of that polarity and the experience of the serene intrinsic purity of nonduality will arise.

By taking the bliss of male and female buddha-union as the path the experience of nondual bliss and emptiness arises.

The 100 Syllable Vajrasattva Mantra

Recite the 100-syllable mantra multiple times, beginning the recitation slowly and ending quickly, and completing each session with Vajrasattva's root mantra.

Recite according to the Tibetan phonetics transcribed from Dudjom Rinpoche's copy that was written in his own hand for his followers:

OM BENZA SA TTO SA MA YA
MA NU PA LA YA
BEN ZA SA TTO TE NO PA TI STHTA
DRI DHO ME BHA WA
SU TO SYO ME BHA WA
SU PO SYO ME BHA WA
A NU RA KTO ME BHA WA
SA RWA SI DDHI ME PRA YA CHHA
SA RWA KA RMA SU CHA ME
CHI TTAM SRE YAH KU RU HUNG
HA HA HA HA HOH
BHA GA WAN SA RWA TA THA GA TA
BEN ZE MA ME MUN CHA
BEN ZE BHA WA
MA HA SA MA YA SA TTO AH

OM BEN ZA SA TTO AH

The Tsikdun Seven Line Prayer

The Seven Line Prayer is far from Dzogchen nonmeditation. It is included here because many radical Dzogchen practitioners will know it by heart and recall it with enthusiasm and joy. Those qualities can be very useful in dissolving impediments to nonmeditation.

HŪNG ! ORGYEN YŪL-KYI NŪP-CHANG TSAM,
PEMA KESAR DONG-PO LA,
YA-TSEN CHOG-KI NGODRŪP NYE,
PEMA JŪNGNE ZHE-SŪ TRAK,
KHORDŪ KHANDRO MANGPO KOR.
KHYE-KYI JEYSU DAG-DRŪB KYE,
CHIN-KYI LOB-CHIR SHEKSŪ SOL,
GŪRŪ PEMA SIDDHI HŪNG.

OM AH HŪNG BENZA GŪRŪ PEMA SIDDHI HŪNG.

HŪNG [invokes the mind of Guru Rinpoche].
In the northwest of the country of Oddiyana,
Born on the pollen bed of a lotus,
Endowed with the most marvellous attainment,
Renowned as the Lotus-Born, Padmasambhava,
Surrounded by a retinue of many Dakinis –
Following you I sing this song,
Please come to bless us.

Master (GŪRŪ) Padmasambhava (PEMA), please bestow (HŪNG) attainments (SIDDHI) [upon us]

The Vajra Song

Chant the Vajra Song of Chogyel Namkhai Norbu:

IV Inspiration and Direction

These extracts, taken primarily from Tulku Pema Rigdzin's magisterial work, The Great Secret of Mind (Snow Lion), *are intended to guide the meditating yogin/yogini in the trekcho sitting practice. Different points of view produce slightly differing models. These excerpts have been edited, to occasionally replace the hortative or conditional mood with the simple present continuative tense.*

The Disposition of the Body

First, you take a comfortable seat, cross-legged, hands in meditation posture, spine straight like an arrow, shoulders held back like a vulture's wings, neck slightly hooked, tongue held against the palate and with the eyes lowered. When you can apply these seven instructions of Vairochana in your meditation, then with a straight spine your energy channels are straightened. If the energy channels are straight, then the movements of energy within the body are quietened, and with energy pacified the mind is luminescent.

The Bones of Dzogchen Practice

People who are not interested in elaborate methods or who are unable to practice them can use this instruction from *The Super-Refined Oral Precepts* of Pema Lingpa, which is eminently portable and extremely potent in its blessings.

Then the Dakini Yeshe Tsogyel requested her master Padma-sambhava to give her simple instructions that condense the teaching into easy practice. The Guru replied, 'Listen, you attractive, devoted, and joyful being! There are many instructions on posture, but just sit relaxed and at ease – that's the essential point. There are many precepts concerning speech and energy, like binding the breath and reciting mantras, but just be silent like a mute – that's the main thing. There are many key points of mind to follow, like fixating the mind, relaxation, radiating and absorbing light, concentration and many others, but just stay free and easy without trying to change anything, just resting naturally – that's the crucial instruction.

Let the body rest like a corpse, without movement; keep silent like a mute; let the mind be, don't change a thing. Let pure presence shine, unmodified, just as it is. Relax, at ease, hang loosely in the natural state.

That is the best way to hold body, speech and mind... There simply is no better method than that...People today are happy and easy in this type of practice. Whatever may be your practice, however, whether short or extensive, it is crucial that you completely understand the view of the Great Perfection.

Sustaining the Awareness of Intrinsic Presence

In his *Wish-Fulfilling Treasury* Longchenpa says,

You sit cross-legged upon a comfortable cushion, take refuge, and recall the bodhisattva vow. Then, the mind focuses loosely on an object of perception, without any idea in mind, without any thought, distraction-free, radiant and shining, and you stay there without concentration or dispersion for an instant. The object of perception is not externalized, you are free of thought, and material objects and the immaterial grasping mind are not dualized. The mind that meditates neither affirms nor negates; what is in front of the mind is said to be absent, for there is nothing there established. Each separate non-referential perception is equal in the immaculate primal awareness of intrinsic presence.

During informal contemplation between sessions of meditation, you recognize appearances as apparent yet non-existent, like magical illusion, and perform dedication and aspiration prayers for the sake of the six classes of sentient beings, all of whom have been our parents. During informal contemplation between sessions, without even a tit of desire, attachment or clinging to the illusory appearances of this life, you may perform prostration and circumambulation, read texts, make tsatsas, water offering and so on.

Maintaining Pure Presence

The pure presence that was introduced in the view is itself the meditation.

Wherever a single perception falls, you let it hang loosely but firmly, without modifying it in any way, and it rests in naked empty pure presence. When you cannot stay therein due to the sudden arising of thought, you just hang loosely in that thought. As creativity the thought is then released into its own ground, like a wave falling back into the ocean, and buddha is recognized in alpha-purity. Engaging diligently and one-pointedly in this practice you are confident, and with creativity optimized constancy is attained.

The Meditation Session

[Then the Guru melts into light and dissolves into us, and his mind becomes inseparable from your own, like water being poured into water; in that space, without modification, relaxed, sustain the view. Alternatively, at this time you can pray to your Guru and Padmasambhava as one, letting the mind stay easy and relaxed, looking at the luminosity of pure presence. Then, when a thought suddenly arises, you can use either method, and relax into it, just as it is.]

With neither affirmation nor rejection, whatever arises in the objective field as a thought form does not crystallize, is not pursued, left unmodified. It is naked pure presence, shining and vivid, with neither projection nor absorption; thus, slowly, pure presence recognizes itself, and you rest in the stillness of the stream of it.

Again, when thought arises, you see its very essence as before and it rests in its natural state, free of acceptance and rejection as good or bad, and free of desire and aversion and so forth. You do not follow thought or suppress it like ordinary worldly people, or like lower approach monks who account thought as sin, denying particular thoughts or transforming them somehow. You do nothing whatsoever, abiding in the natural state.

When you sustain that practice for days, months or years, pure presence is the automatic constant. External conditions do not change it and whatever thoughts arise does so as meditation and dissolves into themselves. You have a built-in trust in our meditation. You have no need of other people's input because meditation is the natural state of things, and you know instinctively with total assurance that no buddha other than the nature of mind exists.

Longchenpa's Precise Instruction

First, in formal meditation, you hang loosely, relaxed, with open natural clarity. You do not label or describe our sensory perception; in that way no attachment to the primal awareness of naked empty presence can arise. With open cognition of the form in the eye, the sound in the ear, the taste on the tongue, the sensation in the body, and the plethora of positive and negative thoughts in the mind, the six varieties of sensory phenomena are neither concretized nor substantiated in any way, and you know pure presence. You do not follow or run after any object, but abiding in translucent perceptivity, experiencing all forms without hope or fear, never modifying or adulterating perception, never rejecting any appearance, whatever arises is released by itself. The mind that apprehends apparent objects in this way is reflexively released in a nonduality of subject and object.

Whatever appears in informal contemplation the gap between meditation sessions should be understood to be like one of the eight metaphors of magical illusion; and thus you are released from desire, hatred, and all emotional affliction. When positive or negative mental display arises, convinced that it is without root or base, neither fixate upon it nor reject it.

Meditation: 'Drawing in Water'

It is surely true that, as for us all, thoughts run continuously, one after the other, like ripples on a pond, and if each thought is to be caught and rejected, one after the other, then even though you practice for an aeon you will not eradicate them all. Whatever thoughts arise you let them arise; and when they have arisen you do not cling to them but let them disappear just as a line drawn in water vanishes the moment after it is inscribed. Letting thoughts disappear immediately into their own pure presence is the Dzogchen mode.

Gaze at the Freshness

If you put all of this concisely, no matter what the quality of the view, whether you are happy or sad, whether appearances are fearful or pleasant, whether mind is active or passive, *you do not tilt our mind towards any antidote.* Whatever appears, you look nakedly at the essence of the appearance as it arises, and, without modifying it in any way, you just let it be. Then pure presence in all its clarity arises from within.

In his *Life-blood of the Mountain Retreat* Dudjom Rinpoche says,

Whatever the sensory field, whatever the object, you gaze at it like a child enrapt before an altar in a temple. You don't clutch the sensory specifics – you hold to the freshness. Let it be in its own place without contriving anything about it, without changing its shape or complexion and without adulterating it with any conceptual fixations. Then all appearances will arise as the naked primal awareness of clarity and emptiness in pure presence.

Guardians of the Dharmakaya: Familiarity

It is not enough merely to look into the space of happiness or sadness; it is important to have pure presence as a constant in that flow. The power of meditation is a constant, and it is impossible not to remain long in the place of nondual perception.

Thoughts arising intermittently will break the continuity, and like ripples on a pond the poisonous taste of emotion arises to obstruct the meditation. Gross thoughts increasing, ripples become rough waves that intensify the emotion. Until subtle emotions are left behind you cannot eradicate suffering, so it is crucially important to sustain the state of meditation.

When you gain a strong familiarity by staying in that space for a long time, whatever thoughts arise, whether gross or subtle, they will dislodge us; upon recognition of the first thought, whatever thought it may be, in that very moment it is realized to be the play of the spontaneous creativity of dharmakaya. Like a wave falling back into the ocean, the thought vanishes into the dharmakaya. In that space of naked empty pure presence that is the view, always cherishing thoughts of the five poisonous emotions and all the movements of body, speech and mind, and the acts of eating, sleeping, moving and sitting, you are known as the yogis and yoginis who stand guard over the shifting dharmakaya display. This is the supreme method of sustaining the essence of meditation. According to the teachings of the Great Perfection, this is unadulterated by any kind of focus; it is called 'the great meditation which is non-meditation'.

The River Flow Training

In short, abandoning yourself completely to whatever arises, no antidotal practice of any kind is necessary. Totally relaxed, gazing into the arising, clear and pure presence naturally arises. External confirmation is redundant because confidence wells up from within.

This view, meditation and conduct rolled into one is called the River Flow Training of the Great Perfection. [Patrul Rinpoche]

A Lesson in 'Meditation'

The method of maintaining the view is called 'meditation'. When you know experientially [in the view] that all experience of phenomena is apparent yet non-existent, like magical illusion, then as each separate emotion arises it is free of the need of a separate dose of emptiness as an antidote, because neither the affliction nor the antidote have ever truly existed. Whatever appears, however, should remain loosely in perception just as it is: sustaining that disposition is called meditation.

If someone asks, 'Why in the Great Perfection is meditation called non-meditation?' the answer is that in [*trekcho* simply sitting] all phenomena are seen as space. But how can we 'hold' space as an object of focus? Space has no specific characteristic, so there is nothing to meditate upon. The nature of mind is primordially unborn and free of all conceptual elaboration, so nothing is there. In that way, no difference can be found between the object of meditation and the mind that is meditating: the disposition of mind in its natural state is called 'nonmeditation'.

What is the meaning of 'natural state'? When mind is disturbed by thoughts, its nature becomes unclear in the same way that a pail of dirty water becomes unclear after it has been stirred – you cannot see the bottom of the pail. When mind is kept unmodified in its natural state, like a pellucid pail of water undisturbed, the nature of mind is pure presence. As the reality – or 'suchness' – of all phenomena is ascertained in the view, no need for any scrutiny or investigation of the nature of mind exists, and therefore simply to abide in the natural state of whatever appears is labelled 'meditation'. This nonmeditation, which is the meditational disposition of Dzogchen is the crux of practice. When you stay in nonmeditation without drifting [into thought], all the points of reference of our internal discussion vanish, and the bright pure presence of self-arising primal awareness dawns spontaneously.

Some may say that this is a mind-constructed meditation because it does not go beyond mental experience. But the temporal mind of the ordinary being who is the meditator is not the meditating mind – the meditator is self-arising primal awareness free of all conceptual elaboration. When you hear a sound, although it is the ear that hears it, it is the unmodified sound that is heard; likewise even though it is the mind that meditates, the meditation is free of all elaboration.

But, then, on the other hand, as Ju Mipham says in his *Reply to Refutation*,

The inexpressible nature of being is experienced and understood as a mere general idea by ordinary believers. In the sutras it is called 'the patience that experientially is in total accord with buddha-dharma'. In the tantras it is called 'illustrative primal awareness'. In reality, in short, it is 'the mind that is in accord with the ultimate absolute'.

Hanging Loosely in Pure Presence

When you lose our identity in pure presence you can simply sit for short periods. If you cannot stay relaxed in pure presence for any length of time, you should do it for short periods.

In a single period, sitting in the sevenfold Vairochana posture, you let the mind hang loosely. As stormy thoughts arise and obscure the meditation, you recall the original view of pure presence that is free of conceptual elaboration. Thus our meditation consists of sometimes being aware of the mind's digressions and sometimes resting in its nature, alternately, or according to our necessity. Through repetition of this process the meditation is strengthened and you can rest in pure presence for a longer time each day. When you abide in pure presence, you no longer watch the mind – that phase of practice is completed.

In such meditation, whatever suffering arises, it is experienced like the meeting of an old friend in the middle of a market-place. Whatever scurry of painful thoughts arise, in the very moment of their appearance those thoughts are known as baseless and rootless, arising and vanishing automatically. No matter how great the pain, when it is experienced in the timeless moment of pure presence, it is known as happiness.

There is no need to confirm this with anyone else for you experience it yourselves. Further, you should look into the nature of mind not just when you suffer but also when you are happy. When happiness is seen as a concrete thing, then attachment gradually increases and, in this way, becomes the root of suffering.

The Three Modes of Release

When a beginner-yogi sees a thought arising he recognizes it as a long-lost friend. Coincident with the arising of a thought, happy or sad, good or bad, is the recognition that the thought is the creativity of pure presence, that it is subjective illusion, and that it is released as it stands. In the middle of the practice, when meditation has improved, the thought releases itself like a snake uncoiling. Whatever happiness or suffering arises in mind, simultaneously with the arising it dissolves into the matrix of pure presence, where joy is free of hope and sorrow is free of fear. Finally, when the meditation is complete, neither sense of benefit nor detriment accompanies any thought, and, therefore, you are like a thief entering an empty house. Whatever negative situation arises cannot disturb us, cannot affect us, and we feel like children gazing at the Madonna.

V The Reason for Daily Practice

This is a rendition of a talk given on Zoom during the early stages of the Covid pandemic. It is more panegyric than prescriptive, featuring Dzogchen as a state complete and perfect as we are, with nothing left to do except follow the dictates of universal necessity (the bodhisattva vow). The daily practice, then, is presented as a celebration not a means to an end, although sometimes it may mistakenly appear otherwise.

Dzogchen stresses basic realization, conviction, and confidence, but we must consider secondary – what some of us need to demote – namely ritual sitting practice. Why should formal meditation be subordinate? Because Dzogchen is a 24-hour a day realization, constant and intensive, while simply sitting is just a part of the daily round. The sitting ritual inevitably puts Dzogchen into objective focus, and we need to do that occasionally - some people need it daily or for extended periods of time – but essentially sitting meditation is of no greater import than drinking a cup of tea. I will talk about that at length and the attitude with which we can include the sitting ritual into the 24-hour meditation most effectively. But remember, simply sitting has no greater significance than anything else that we do. When we make sitting meditation a cause (or an effect) of a higher mental state, we are no longer celebrating the immediacy and the natural immanence of Dzogchen, the great perfection, and awareness of it as life and lifestyle, but rather reinforcing a sense of insufficiency.

Recognition of the value of simply sitting is recognition of the futility of doing anything at all in pursuit of the Great Perfection. The purpose of simply sitting meditation is no purpose at all. An understanding of this conundrum depends on an initial hit of the real thing – the initiatory realization. But we can't simply sit with the purpose of attaining no purpose. No-purpose must be built-in. No-purpose was realized in initiatory experience, and simply sitting is a re-enactment of that experience of the nature of mind, or the recall of it. But experience of mind's nature has no particular quality or sign so that anything and everything that arises in the simply sitting practice, just as in the duration of the inter-session experience, is IT and requires no modification or change. Simply sitting is demonstration of the Dzogchen view.

We may initially define the Dzogchen view from the inside looking out, but that perspective is provisional and, although functional in balancing the ignorant dualized view of looking inwards from the outside, it is equally as partial and therefore foolish. The Dzogchen view, the view that we naturally fall into with experience of mind's nature is the nondual view that abhors the extremes of identifying with either inner or outer perspective. The inner identification reifies, or substantiates, the center of the mandala as the 'I' that is separate from the forms that arise as expression of it. This may be considered a 'higher' vision of reality than the dualized vision of looking in from the outside, but it still implies a dualization. Our simply sitting implies a nondual view in which the subjective and objective aspects are equal and interfused so that there is no cognitive differential. Simply sitting is the practice of simply being, in which the restrictions of the mandala's parameters have disappeared.

In our nondual mandala, experience, which may be redefined as ordinary everyday perception fully illuminated, we have a 360-degree perspective in which everything falls into its natural place, with every specific possessing total meaning like seeing the universe in a grain of sand, where every timeless moment is a completion, a fulfillment. The bodhisattva vow naturally manifests therein. We have given up the idea of passing through a doorway from a lower to a higher state, and also the idea of a key that can unlock a door that leads into a higher interior reality, because we are already there, not merely in a higher reality but in the absolute reality, grounded in the experience of mind's nature that includes both inside and outside. This is the fundamental intuition that we can stake on in this lifetime. When we acknowledge this as reality it becomes the illusion of daily life, and we are content with that puzzle, and no aspect of it has more value than any other – it is all light and bright and happy. Unless and until we have an intimation of this realization and appropriate conviction along with it, simply sitting is counter-productive. Or maybe the form of it that you practice belongs to another discipline, like the gradual path in Vajrayana, where we try to improve our mindset, trying to see the colors of existence, trying to improve the relative condition of our life – that is something else, like religion maybe. What we are looking at here and now in simply sitting is acknowledgement of the default in every mode of existence, in every moment of experience, or to put it another way, simple realization, recognition, re-experience of the nature of mind – that's all.

In both the short and long forms of ritual Dzogchen, the essential practice is simply sitting – by doing nothing at all ritually, we remember the natural identification with mind's nature. It is just ritual, and once the posture is established – and that itself is simply sitting – by playing that nothing is done, by imitating reality, we recall initiatory experience and re-establish Dzogchen as the natural state of being. The dictatorial mind that has told us to sit and do nothing through that admonition has abandoned its role as goal-setter and attainer, the 'how to do better' imperative has been left behind. Doing nothing is what simply sitting implies: ritual abandonment of the self-directed dictates of the discursive mind – at least for the duration of the session. What we call the 'will' cannot actualize the nature of mind because that actualization is an automatic function of being, but by creating an absence it can sharpen the recollection of mind's nature so that it remains in mind for the remainder of the 24-hour day. Literally doing nothing, we clarify the identity with the nature of mind and by so doing, metaphorically, we do nothing. Reawakening, sharpening, our identity as mind's nature, we are free from attachment with whatever arises during the session and also after getting up from it.

Once the Dzogchen view is established in the root of the mind in simply sitting, we *remain* in the root of the mind between sessions. That root is the source of light and awareness. Or to put it another way, doing nothing in ritual simply sitting is setting ourselves up for the total energization, resuscitation, or recognition of mind's nature both in the ritual process and in the gaps between sessions. Does the ritual setting actually induce experience of heightened awareness? Does the ritual guarantee a moment of temporal enlightenment? Of course not, but it sets us up for recall of the nature of mind or for resolution of conditions that obstruct clarity. Or to put it another way, the drive, the ambition, to attain enlightenment is lost in simple appreciation of the here and now. The 'intentionality', as a dynamic function of the will, an egoic mechanism entailing a causal process, dissolves. In the absence of this positive thrust, a nonstate of nonaction prevails, opening to the 24-hour nonmeditation.

When we identify with the nature of mind in this way, *allowing* spontaneity, the discursive mental function is demoted. We can now focus on the full scope of incoming sensory information, and along with the spontaneity comes automatic fulfillment of the bodhisattva vow, an absence of distinction between self and other, and automatic responsiveness to what is beneficial for all. It implies a minimum of attention paid to the temporal intellectual commentary – the less attachment to that commentary the more identified we are with the nondual root. The immediacy of the situation is all.

The graduated path is driven by goals: here in immediacy – on the immediate path – the nature of mind provides intrinsic trust in spontaneous response, and simultaneously in confidence in the purpose of being. This intrinsic sense of immediacy is the hallmark of Dzogchen. However, the graduated path inculcates a hierarchy of form, an intellectual perspective, that creates a difference between the blissed-out yogin and the socially-conscious, bodhisattva-lama. Perhaps we need a bit of the social awareness that is inculcated on the graduated path. In the immediate situation it appears as needed in a karmically determined form. It's like, pure immediate Dzogchen is only 99.99% of buddha's mandala – the outstanding 0.01% is the Dzogchen social form.

The simply-sitting component of the 24-hour meditation takes precedence over all other ritual postures comprising the day. It doesn't matter where you are or what time it is, just relax into the nature of mind when you feel the urge or the need. But doing it at a particular time of the day provides a frame in which memory can work for us. Remember the teaching that Guru Rinpoche gives to Yeshe Tsogyel: he said something like, 'Sit like a sack of potatoes and keep silent. Allow each and every thought to arise but don't do anything about it.' That is the essence of ritual non-action in sitting. You can call it practice if you like, because we are rehearsing what we are going to do in every moment thereafter, but as soon as possible let go of that intellectual overview because we are actually experiencing the manifold rainbow nature of mind in all its splendor in the here and now, and there is nothing but the here and now – time is shot!

Everything in the ritual – the sitting, the silence – is subordinate to the awareness. The form is secondary, almost irrelevant, and that's why it can be called ritual. Don't consider the main thing to be taking the ritual seat and the 'correct' posture of the body, but rather understand that the crux of the ritual is in the awareness of mind. Identify with the heart-center, and then the form and thought and the body on the seat, in the room, in the house, in the country, on the planet becomes ornamental detail. Thus the awareness takes on the ritual form and cannot be separated from it. The form of the ritual becomes extended into every moment of being in the body and particularly in the gaps between simply sitting following the movement of the body – the specific moment by moment movement of the body. The body is in a process of constant change, always changing from one precise particular to the next. Such is the ritual when we get up in the morning wash, eat and shit: it is all ritual. The simply siting is just another element of it and we don't leave the ritual behind when we get up from the cushion. Overtly, ritual is repetition, vibrating in a particular way, expression of the same habitual vibration and sound, but actually every moment of ritual is new and fresh and can never be repeated because that is the nature of awareness.

Simply sitting is in that way the form of ritual practice. Sit in front of an altar if you like, it may provide inspiration. Make some offering, it's fun and if you enjoy it, that's great, but it's not necessary. If we need reminding of the priority of interiority and the dominance of Mind, it may introduce a red herring. If we are happy in the equivalence of inside and outside, we certainly don't need a ritual representation on an altar. The real 'altar' is the spaciousness that underlies all perception where the offerings are the sensory objects that enter consciousness. We need *to know* those offerings, that is essential, but in daily life we don't have to represent them, externally. The question is, do we need external reminders?

Should we do the long or short form of the ritual practice? Simply sitting is certainly the essence of both. The short form gives the opportunity for the simple ritual essence. The long form provides various ritual opportunities to welcome that essence of mind and to assist in sliding through particularly intransigent moments. Both long and short begin with the simple ritual of the nine breaths which put the bodymind in gear. Wake up and do the Nine Breaths! It's the wake-up call common to all dharma practitioners. Perhaps you already do something similar and know the value of it.

The Refuge is fundamental and central. It is the moment when we formally evoke the nature of mind and existentially re-cognize – remember – the ground of being. The ground of being is the essential nature of life – the basic element – and we use a symbolic shout to re-cognize it. 'Shout of recognition' is a description of the syllable HŪNG and the sound HŪNG is a symbolic recognition of the nature of mind. Repetition of the syllable HŪNG is the mantra of the nature of the Guru, both at rest and in dynamic motion. The HŪNG recalls initiatory experience and that is the root cause of the sanctity of the HŪNG – it represents the primary point of being, our moment of recognition, our identity with the nondual nature of mind.

Inherent in that recognition of the nature of mind is the *bodhichitta*, the cradle of the bodhisattva vow. That vow is not something that the guru imposes; it comes from within, it leaps up and out and then we can't do anything else but bodhisattvic activity. We have no choice. It is not like a command from outside that has to be obeyed, or an agenda that we produce after deep thought. Immersed in the nature of mind it is second nature. We use the sound HO as symbolic recognition of this great active aspect of being and its purpose which is summed up as the bodhisattva vow.

Simply sitting comes after the HŪNG and the HO. Technically, simply sitting is classified as *trekcho* – Breakthrough – meditation. In latterday development of the Nyingma approach to their changeless non-meditation, two schools were developed – *trekcho* and *togal*. In recent centuries Nyingma lamas were caught by these technical – or perhaps 'academic' is a better word – terms signifying somewhat different approaches to the same essential reality that is clarified in the simply sitting. Under the headings *trekcho* and *togal* interesting pointers and techniques are included that allow space for the nature of mind to shine through, although insofar as we get into technique we are no longer doing Dzogchen – Vajrayana is the reservoir of technique. Recognizing identity as the nature of mind is our sole concern. *Trekcho* and *togal* provide key mnemonic strategies for getting into the Dzogchen gear – into the nature of mind – which we already know but through a glass darkly.

The indications – I say 'indications' rather than 'instruction' as in 'things to be done' – are introduced in the initiatory ritual made by the initiating lama in the seminal *trekcho* ritual initiation of Creative Presence (*rigpaitsel-wong*). These indications are not a list of things that the student must *do* but rather a statement of how he/she actually *is*. This state is reflected in terms of four substantive notions – 'mountain', 'ocean', 'appearances' and '*rigpa*' – not as characteristics to develop but as intimations of what the nature of mind *is*, and for what is involuntarily recognized in the moment. These intimations – in the form of two metaphors and two abstract nouns – are ideas that provide perspective. When these ideas are introduced formally, the first describes view, the second meditation (nonmeditation), the third activity and the fourth the totality.

The fourth, *rigpa*, is the single expression that may define and encompass the nature of mind. We translate it as 'pure presence'. Although the root of the word means 'knowing', in the Dzogchen context it comprehends the unitary subject/object momentary nondual sensory experience. *Rigpa* overcomes – overwhelms – the intellect; the intellect can't get itself around *rigpa*. When we think '*rigpa*', if we know the real meaning, then the intellect dissolves and we fall into the nature of mind.

The manner of introducing simply sitting is important. Simply sitting comes with freedom from intellectual determinacy, which may be restated as without accepting and without rejecting whatever arises in the mind. When we watch without intellectual concern, free of discrimination, we fall into the awareness that is inherent in total identity with what is going on, full awareness of the incoming sensory information. In that way discursive thought – along with its associated emotion – is marginalized, sidelined, even trivialized. This awareness, identified as the only 'real' element of knowledge is elevated to a super-awareness status, a nondual awareness that is best described as knowledge of itself. It is certainly not a subjective knower grasping a substantial object. Here is 'total identity', or nonduality; it is awareness with/without separation – surely the best poetry and music tries to reproduce that effect.

We can see why the simply sitting does not have any fixed or preferred ritual duration: both the 20-minute and multiple-hour session are permeated by the nature of mind – whether we recognize it or not – just as the gaps between sessions are likewise permeated by the nature of mind . Does the duration of the sitting session affect the possibility of recognition? Get up and go on with the day and we have the same possibility of recognition of the nature of mind. So what does simply sitting provide in terms of potential for realizing the nature of mind? Surely it sharpens the listening mudra that is a constant during the entire 24 hours. What is 'heard' is either the nature of mind in its lucidity or in its opacity and as long as it is 'heard' its color doesn't matter.

What benefit do the long-session exercises have in the Dzogchen moment? Surely they are the scrumptious fruit of being alive, but looking at sensory experience as ideas, there is always a screen of maya, transparent or opaque before our eyes. When the screen is translucent the nature of mind is vividly apparent; when the screen is opaque, when 'we can't see the light', only shadowy forms being visible, we tend habitually to deny that light. But absence of light is also light and when through identity with – and experience of – mind's nature we have a basic assurance that the light is always there, sitting and not sitting produce identical results.

Access to the nature of mind cannot be lost or found. Neither long nor short sessions provide access because we never lost that access, but it can give clarity to sensory experience *as* the nature of mind.

The first *ngondro* exercise, the vajra-standing-posture, clarifies the mind and stops – or integrates – thought. In the vajra-sitting-posture awareness is sharpened. It is a yoga posture.

But let's pass on quickly to the vital breathing exercises known as 'clarification of energy'. This exercise – or better call it a *yoga* – doesn't require anything except insight into ordinary mind. Increase the depth of breathing, marginally extend the length of inbreath and outbreath, suffuse the breathing with the syllable HŪNG and we are looking at the breath riding on its essential nature. The nature of the breath is symbolized and visualized as the syllable HŪNG. The syllable HŪNG is not just a form to be visualized in the sky; it is a nondual, multi-levelled experience. We are identifying the breath with the HŪNG. Does that imply 'de-objectification' of the breath, or perhaps 'projecting' awareness into the breath and *recognizing* the breath? 'Awareness' (*yeshe*) is simply a pointing counter, part of a language that doesn't describe anything substantial or even notional; it is a metaphor for the light of the mind and is indicated symbolically by the HŪNG. The HŪNG provides recollection of the awareness of the nature of mind that was imbued by initiatory experience, the constant experience that provides identity with the nondual essence – the nonduality of emptiness and form. This can be expressed existentially as '*in* experience but not *of* it'.

The HŪNG breathing uses the eyes (the 'far-reachers') together with the breath, and the breath is projected into the 360-degree vertical mandala of visual form (or is it a half-globe?). The HŪNGs represent the nonobjectifiable cognitive essence of the experience. The discursive memory-stuff that our intellectual intelligence projects into visual experience is left behind – it is only the *nature* of experience that remains. On the outbreath, seeing the world as color, momentarily we are free of karma; on the inbreath, seeing the innate purity of the subjective entity (body-mind), then the karma of our embodiment if not eradicated is at least shaken up.

Awareness of mind when it is at rest, that is the blue HŪNG; awareness of mind when it is enlivened in a potentially active body, that is the red HŪNG. That wrathful, dynamic HŪNG, the HŪNG that gives light to the energetic mind, the intensely consuming red HŪNG, burns out excremental attachment.

The clarification of energy through breathing is done by means of recognition of its essential nature. The mental clarification, therefore, is perhaps the more efficacious of these supportive exercises. These mental exercises are called 'clarification of mind' rather than 'purification of mind' because the word the more literal translation of the Tibetan in this context evokes the common dualistic-moralistic Christian association. 'Clarity', rather than 'purity', is the ultimate quality of mind.

In this supportive exercise, clarification of mind is synonymous with 'clarification of thought' and the principal element of the clarification of mind is to look into thought as it arises, not at the logical meaning of the thought but at the substantial nature of the thought. Looking into a single thought as it arises – looking into the nature of mind – frees us not only from attachment to the primary semantic meaning of the thought but also from all the baggage that the thought brings along with it, the associations that we have amassed in a lifetime, and its social and human aspects, all of it arisen from the dualization of reality apparent in the form of the thought. Looking at the clarity of the thought (which in philosophical Buddhism is called 'emptiness') relieves us of the weight of association and gives us identity with the nature of mind. The nature of mind is by definition free of karmic determinants. In this way 'all-being' (*samanta-bhadra*) is allowed to express itself as part of the universal picture, as a pixel in the totality.

The crucial element in these clarification exercises is the 'release factor'. The release factor kicks in automatically when we identify with the fundamental awareness of the nature of mind. Like that awareness, it cannot be consciously induced. Like the immediate and automatic dissolution of a figure drawn in water, given an absence of attachment to sensory perception release is reflexive. Such release provides conviction in nonaction and the confidence that releases is inherent in the basic nature of mind. It is the absence of attachment that allows it. The thoughts that arise and fall in the here and now – are released from gross attachment to the samsara of the moment and the sticky multi-dimensional world. When we look into a thought as it arises we are home free because thought is all we have by which sensory impressions may be recognized. It is said that there is nothing in dharma more important than recognition of this automatic release factor. Release (liberation) is our over-riding existential concern – it is what changes a life of constant painful obsession into a life of pleasure and joy. It is what we wish our children to be aware of from the beginning – it makes life so much easier and happier for them.

These clarification exercises need time and energy. They allow the nature of mind to shine through more than in other karmas, if only for the reason that the disruptive discursive, comparative, function is dormant. The essential insight has the same potential in the long form of meditation as in the short form. Simply being is being here and now without egoic intellectual prodding. The nature of mind is naturally enshrined in this body-mind; it is not separate from us, and it is ever-present in a state of constant change.

Whether it is short or long, these simply sitting practices end with the Dedication ritual that stresses the recognition that Dzogchen is for the universe, for all sentient beings, out of universal necessity. It is a restatement of our awareness of the bodhisattva vow inherent in the nature of mind. We make this statement of recognition at the end of the simply sitting practice because the universe demands it, because the universe is a totality of which we are an integral part. The dedication is recognition of the part we play in the totality, the recognition of the universe in a grain of sand, the smallest part identified with the whole.

The Dzogchen view is clearly not philosophical Buddhism, and Dzogchen meditation doesn't require buddhist tantric method. But just as the King cannot rule except by his Court – the President by his Congress – so Dzogchen expresses itself through Buddhism. So don't think that because we have discovered Dzogchen that Buddhism is redundant – as Padmasambhava allegedly said, 'Reduce karma to its ultimate triturated constituent and you find the nature of mind.'

Dzogchen Teaching Series

Radical Dzogchen: Available on Amazon

Nonmeditation
Semdzins
The Dzogchen View
SAMAYA
Khorde Rushen
Daily Practice
Mahamudra
Pilgrimage
Bardo
Mandala
Karuna

www.ingramcontent.com/pod-product-compliance
Ingram Content Group UK Ltd.
Pitfield, Milton Keynes, MK11 3LW, UK
UKHW040012200726
13854UKWH00001B/164

9 798689 195858